INDIAN QUEENS

BRAVE INDIAN QUEENS

SUNDARAM DUBEY

Contents

ONE
RANI ABBAKKA CHOWTA

In Dakshina Kannada's Bantwal taluk, a historian has erected a museum in the memory of a 16th-century warrior queen. The man behind the museum, called Tulu Baduku Museum, is Prof. Thukaram Poojary and his subject is Rani Abbakka Chowta of Ullal.

The only woman in history to confront, fight and repeatedly defeat the Portuguese, Rani Abbakka's unflagging courage and indomitable spirit are at par with the legendary Rani Laxmi Bai of Jhansi, Rani Rudramma Devi of Warangal and Rani Chennamma of Kittur. Yet, little is written about her or her incredible story in the history books.

Since the 7th century, maritime trade (in spices, textiles, war horses etc) had flourished between the communities of India's western coast and the Arabian Peninsula. With an eye on this lucrative trade, several European powers had been trying to discover the sea route to India. The Portuguese finally became the first Europeans to find a sea route to India when Vasco Da Gama reached Calicut in 1498 after a long voyage.

Five years later, the Portuguese built their first fort at Cochin. This was followed by the establishment of a ring of forts in the Indian Ocean region – in India, Muscat, Mozambique, Sri Lanka, Indonesia, even as far as Macau in China.

his, along with its superior naval technology, put the control of all the spice routes to India into the hands of the Portuguese within twenty years of Da Gama's historic voyage.

For the whole of the 16th century, Portuguese dominance in the region remains unchallenged by any other European power (the Dutch, the French and the British reached India only at the start of the 17th century).

Trading in the Indian Ocean, which had hitherto been a free trade zone for Indian, Arab, Persian and African ships, now required a paid permit (cartaz) from the Portuguese. The naval superiority of the Portuguese meant that they invariably won against local rulers who rebelled.

In 1526, the Portuguese captured the Mangalore port. Their next target was Ullal, a thriving port town that lay nestled between the verdant peaks of the Western Ghats and the cerulean blue waters of the Arabian Sea.

Ullal was the capital of the Chowta king Thirumala Raya III. Feudatories of the Vijayanagar kingdom, the Chowtas were Jain kings who had originally migrated to Tulu Nadu (a province consisting of present-day Dakshina Kannada district of Karnataka, portions of Udupi and Kasargod district in Kerala) from Gujarat in the 12th century.

As the Chowtas were a matrilineal dynasty, the king's heir was his young niece, Abbakka. The fiercely independent princess had been trained in sword fighting, archery, cavalry, military strategy, diplomacy and all other subjects of statecraft from a very young age. As such, when Abbakka was crowned the Queen of Ullal, she was deeply aware of the threat posed by the Portuguese presence on the coast and equally determined to resist it with all she had.

Before his death, Thirumala Raya III had arranged a strategic marriage alliance for Abbakka with Lakshmappa Bangaraja, the ruler of Mangalore. As the ruler of Ullal, Rani Abbakka continued to live in her own home even after marriage and the couple's three children stayed with her. However, the marriage broke down when Bangaraja compromised with the Portuguese.

With an eye on Ullal's trade (that had flourished under the Queen's able leadership), the Portuguese had been trying to exact tributes and taxes from Rani Abbakka. Incensed and exasperated at the unfair demands, she refused to accede to the Portuguese demands.

Her ships continued to trade with the Arabs despite attacks by the Portuguese. From Mogaveeras and Billava archers to Mappilah oars men, people of all castes and religions found a place in her army and navy.

Infuriated by her effrontery, the Portuguese began attacking Ullal repeatedly.The first battle took place in the year 1556, with the Portuguese fleet being commanded by Admiral Don Alvaro de Silveira, and ended in an uneasy truce.

Two years later, the Portuguese attacked with a larger force and were able to ransack the settlement at Ullal to some extent. However, Rani

Abbakka's masterful battle tactics and diplomatic strategy (she collaborated with Arab Moors and Zamorin of Kozhikode) pushed them back once again.

During the next battle, the Portuguese army under General Joao Peixoto attacked Ullal and managed to capture the royal palace. However, Rani Abbakka escaped before they could capture her.

Along with 200 loyal soldiers, she raided the Portuguese in the dead of night and killed the general along with 70 of his soldiers. Frightened by the ferocity of the attack, the remaining Portuguese troops fled to their ships

By this time, the Portuguese had become alarmed about Rani Abbakka's growing reputation inspiring other rulers. When repeated frontal attacks didn't work, they resorted to treachery. A series of edicts were passed to make any alliance with the defiant queen illegal. Her husband, Bangaraja of Mangalore, was also warned against sending any aid to Ullal under the threat of burning his capital.

Yet, Rani Abbakka continued to dismiss these rulings with contempt and scorn. The stunned Portuguese now decided to send Anthony D' Noronha (the Portuguese Viceroy of Goa) to attack Ullal. In 1581, 3000 Portuguese troops supported by an armada of battleships attacked Ullal in a surprise pre-dawn attack.

Rani Abbakka was returning from a visit to her family temple and was caught off guard but she immediately mounted her horse and rode into the battle, leading her troops in a fierce counter-offensive.

Her piercing battle cry – "Save the motherland. Fight them on land and the sea. Fight them on the streets and the beaches. Push them back to the waters", echoed through winds as she and her soldiers fired flaming arrows at the Portuguese ships.

While many of the ships in the Portuguese armada burnt that night, Rani Abbakka was wounded in the crossfire and was captured by the enemy with the help of a few bribed chieftains. Rebellious till the very end, the fearless queen breathed her last in captivity. However, her legacy lived on through her equally fierce and brave daughters who continued to defend Tulu Nadu from the Portuguese.

A warrior queen who gave her life in defence of her freedom and motherland, Rani Abbakka remained a major thorn in the Portuguese' side throughout her rule despite their superior military power. This itself speaks volumes about her courage and ingenuity. Yet her splendid story remains largely forgotten by history books.

The good news is that the legendary queen of Ullal continues to live on in the folk culture of the Dakshin Kannada region (through Bhuta Kola and Yakshagana). In the recent years, her story has been gradually coming to public attention.

Dakshin Kannada has been holding an annual celebration in her memory (Veera Rani Abbakka Utsava) for the last few years.

And there is also Tulu Baduku museum in Bantwal that displays around 3000 artefacts collected from dusty family attics by Poojary over a period of 20 years. Asked what motivated him to do so, Prof. Poojary explained to DNA,

"As a person who has made a career out of teaching history, I cannot allow an important freedom fighter to be forgotten just like that. Let the generations of future historians derive inspiration from it and dwell deep into Rani Abbakka's life."

TWO

QUEEN AHILYABAI HOLKAR

In latter days from Brahma came,
To rule our land, a noble dame,
Kind was her heart and bright her fame,
Ahilya was her honoured name," writes poet Joanna Baillie in 1849 in honour of one of the greatest Maratha woman rulers of Malwa.

Her father, Mankoji Rao Shinde, was the Patil (chief) of the village. Despite women's education being a far cry in the village, her father homeschooled her to read and write.

While Ahilya did not come from a royal lineage, most deem her entry into history a twist of fate. It dates back to when the acclaimed Lord of the Malwa territory, Malhar Rao Holkar, spotted an eight-year-old Ahilyabai at the temple service feeding the hungry and poor, on his stop in Chaundi while travelling to Pune.

Moved by the young girl's charity and strength of character, he decided to ask her hand in marriage for his son Khanderao Holkar. She was married to Khanderao Holkar in 1733 at the tender age of 8.

But distress was quick to befall the young bride when her husband Khanderao was killed in the battle of Kumbher in 1754, leaving her a widow at only 29.

When Ahilyabai was about to commit Sati, her father-in-law Malhar Rao refused to let it happen.

He had been her strongest pillar of support at the time. But a young Ahilyabai could see her kingdom fall like a pack of cards after her father-in-law passed away in 1766, only 12 years after the death of his son Khanderao.

The old ruler's death led to his grandson and Ahilyabai's only son Male Rao Holkar ascending the throne under her regency.

The last straw came when the young monarch Male Rao too died, a few months into his rule, on 5 April 1767, thus creating a vacuum in the power structure of the kingdom.

One can imagine how a woman, royalty or not, would suffer after losing her husband, father-in-law and only son. But Ahilyabai stood undeterred. She did not let the grief of her loss affect the administration of the kingdom and the lives of her people.

While there was indeed a section of the kingdom that objected to her assumption to the throne, her army of Holkars stood by her and supported their queen's leadership.

Just a year into her rule, one saw the brave Holkar queen protect her kingdom – fighting off invaders tooth and nail from plundering Malwa. Armed with swords and weapons, she led armies into the battlefield.

There she was, the queen of Malwa, slaying her enemies and invaders on battlefronts with four bows and quivers of arrows fitted to the corners of the howdah of her favourite elephant.

Her confidante on military matters was Subhedar Tukojirao Holkar (also Malhar Rao's adopted son) whom she appointed the head of the military.

The Queen of Malwa, apart from being a brave queen and proficient ruler, was also an erudite politician. She observed the bigger picture when the Maratha Peshwa couldn't pin down the agenda of the British.

In her letter to the Peshwa in 1772, she had warned him, calling the British embrace a bear-hug: "Other beasts, like tigers, can be killed by might or contrivance, but to kill a bear it is very difficult. It will die only if you kill it straight in the face, Or else, once caught in its powerful hold; the bear will kill its prey by tickling. Such is the way of the English.

And given this, it is difficult to triumph over them."From a tiny village to a flourishing city, Indore prospered during her 30-year rule. She was famous for having built numerous forts and roads in Malwa, sponsoring festivals and giving donations to many Hindu temples.

The Holkar queen also embellished and beautified various sites including Kashi, Gaya, Somnath, Ayodhya, Mathura, Haridwar, Kanchi, Avanti, Dwarka, Badrinarayan, Rameshwar and Jaganathpuri as recorded by the Bharatiya Sanskritikosh.

Her capital at Maheshwar was a melting pot of literary, musical, artistic and industrial achievements. She opened her capital's doors to stalwarts like Marathi poet Moropant, Shahir Anantaphandi and Sanskrit scholar, Khushali Ram.

Her capital was known for is distinct craftsmen, sculptors and artists who were paid handsomely for their work and kept in high regards by the Queen. She also moved on to establishing a textile industry in the city.

Ahilyabai held public audiences every day to help address the grievances of her people. She was always available to anyone who needed her ear.

Historians write how she encouraged all within her realm and her kingdom to do their best. During her reign, the merchants produced their most elegant clothes and trade flourished to no end. No more was the farmer a mere victim of oppression but a self-sufficient man in his own right.

"Far and wide the roads were planted with shady trees, and wells were made, and rest-houses for travellers. The poor, the homeless, the orphaned were all helped according to their needs. The Bhils, who had long been the torment of all caravans, were routed from their mountain fastnesses and persuaded to settle down as honest farmers. Hindu and Musalman alike revered the famous Queen and prayed for her long life," writes Annie Besant.

A woman ahead of her times, Ahilyabai's greatest sorrow continued to remain the irony that her daughter jumped into the funeral pyre and became a Sati upon the death of her husband, Yashwantrao Phanse.

Indore long mourned its noble Queen, happy had been her reign, and her memory is cherished with deep reverence unto this day," writes Besant.

THREE
RANI CHENNAMMA

Kittur Chennamma, the Queen of Kittur, was one of the first Indian rulers to lead an armed rebellion against the British East India Company in 1824, against the implementation of the Doctrine of Lapse. She was born in 1778, 56 years before the 1857 revolt led by Rani Lakshmi Bai, thus becoming the one of the first women freedom fighters to have fought against the British rule in India.

Her rebellion against the British ended with her imprisonment, however, she became a celebrated freedom fighter in the state of Karnataka and a symbol of the independence movement in India. Since 1824, 'Kittur Utsava' has been organised every year in the month of October to celebrate the heroic rebellion of Rani Kittur Chennamma.

Also Read: Accamma Cherian: The Jhansi Rani Of Travancore | #IndianWomenInHistory

Early Life

[Image Courtesy: Journeys Across Karnataka]

Kittur Chennamma was born on October 23, 1778, in Kakati, a small village in the present Belagavi District of Karnataka, India. She belonged to the Lingayat community and received training in horse riding, sword fighting and archery from a young age. She was well known throughout her village for her bravery.

She was married to Mallasarja Desai, the king of Kittur, at the age of 15 and became the queen of Kittur. She had one son from the marriage, who after the death of her husband in 1816, also died in 1824. As the queen of Kittur, Kittur Chennamma adopted Shivalingappa after the death of her only son with the aim of making him the heir to the throne of Kittur.

Defiance of British Rule

The British East India Company did not take lightly to Chennamma's act and ordered Shivalingappa's exile from the kingdom. This was done under the pretext of the Doctrine of Lapse, according to which adoptive children of native rulers were not allowed to be named their successor and if the native rulers did not have children of their own, their kingdom would become a territory of the British Empire. The Doctrine of Lapse was officially codified between 1848 to 1856 by Lord Dalhousie.

Kittur Chennamma, however, defied the British order to expel Shivalingappa from the throne. She sent a letter to the Governor of Bombay to plead the cause of Kittur but Lord Elphinstone turned down Chennamma's request. The state of Kittur came under the administration of Dharwad collectorate in charge of Mr. Thackeray, and Mr. Chaplin was the commissioner. Both men did not recognise Chennamma as the regent and Shivalingappa as the ruler and apprised Rani Chennamma to surrender her kingdom, but she again defied the British order. This led to the breakout of a war.

Also Read: Begum Samru: Nautch Girl Turned Queen Of Sardhana | #IndianWomenInHistory

War against the British

The British attempted to pillage Kittur's treasures and jewels, which valued around 15 lakh rupees, but were unsuccessful. They had attacked Kittur with a force of 20,000 men and 400 guns, which came mainly from the third troop of the Madras Native Horse Artillery.

[Image Courtesy: Journeys Across Karnataka]

In the first battle between the British and Kittur, on October of 1824, British forces faced heavy losses. St. John Thackeray, the British collector and political agent, was also killed during this first battle by the Kittur forces. Rani Chennamma's lieutenant, Amatur Balappa, was mainly responsible for Thackeray's death and the losses faced by the British forces. Two British officers, Sir Walter Elliot and Mr. Stevenson, were also taken hostages by Rani Chennamma's forces.

To avoid further destruction and war, Rani Chennamma negotiated with the British Commissioner Mr. Chaplin and the Governor of Bombay, under whose regime Kittur fell. She released the hostages owing to the British promise that the war would no longer be continued. However, the promise turned out to be only an act of deception. Humiliated by their first defeat at the hands of a small Indian ruler, Mr. Chaplin treacherously returned with much larger forces from Mysore and Sholapur to attack Kittur once again.

[Image Courtesy: Journeys Across Karnataka]

Rani Chennamma fought the second battle fiercely with the aid of her lieutenant Sangoli Rayanna and Gurusiddappa. During this second round of war, the Sub-collector of Sholapur, Mr. Munrow, nephew of Sir Thomas Munro, was also killed. For 12 days, Chennamma and her soldiers relentlessly defended their fort, but yet again, Chennamma was made prey to deceit. Two soldiers of her own army, Mallappa Shetty and Vankata Rao, betrayed Chennamma by mixing mud and cow dung with the gunpowder used for the canons.

Ultimately, Kittur Chennamma and her forces were outnumbered by the large strength of the British forces. Rani Chennamma was defeated in her last battle and captured by the British, who imprisoned her at the Bailhongal Fort for life.

Her loyal lieutenant Sangoli Rayanna continued the guerrilla war even in her absence up to 1829, but in vain. He wished to install Shivalingappa, Chennamma's adopted son, as the ruler of Kittur, but he was captured and hanged by the British. Shivalingappa was also arrested by the British forces.

Also Read: Razia Sultan: The First and Last Woman Ruler of Delhi Sultanate | #IndianWomenInHistory

Imprisonment and Death

[Image Courtesy: Hindu History]

After being captured, Rani Chennamma spent the last five years of her life in imprisonment at Bailhongal Fort reading holy texts and performing pooja. She took her last breath at the Bailhongal Fort on February 21, 1829.

Rani Chennamma's samadhi (burial place) is in Bailhongal taluk, under the care of Government agencies. However, sadly, the burial place of this valiant queen lies neglected, in a state of poor maintenance. The only time the place is looked after is during the 'Kittur Utsava' and 'Kannada Rajyotsava'.

Commemorations

Kittur Rani Chennamma is still remembered for her valour. Even though she couldn't win the war against the British, she became an inspiration for India's freedom fighters and a lesson for the British government that Indian rulers will not accept their enforced laws without a good fight.

During the freedom movement, her brave resistance against the British forces became the theme of several inspirational plays, folk songs (Lavani) and stories. Rani Chennamma's first victory against the British forces is still honoured annually in October during the 'Kittur Utsava', held in Kittur.

[Image Courtesy: Wikipedia]

A historical-drama film called Kitturu Chennamma was produced and directed by B. R. Panthulu about the life and times of Kittur Rani Chennamma. A popular daily Indian Railways train that connects Bangalore and Kolhapur was also named after her as Rani Chennamma Express.

On September 11, 2007, Rani Chennamma's statue was unveiled at the Indian Parliament complex in New Delhi by the first woman President of India, Smt. Pratibha Patil. The statue was donated by the Kittur Rani Chennamma Memorial Committee and was sculpted by Vijay Gaur. Two other statues of Rani Chennamma were also installed at Bangalore and Kittur.

Tagged Under: #IndianWomenInHistoryKittur ChennammaKittur Rani ChennammaRani Chennamma

FOUR

RANI DURGAVATI

Rani Durgavati was born on 5th October 1524 A.D. in the family of famous Chandel emperor Keerat Rai. She was born at the fort of Kalanjar(Banda, U.P.). Chandel Dynasty is famous in the Indian History for the valiant king Vidyadhar who repulsed the attacks of Mehmood Gaznavi. His love for sculptures is shown in the world famed temples of Khajuraho and Kalanjar fort. Rani Durgavati's achievements further enhanced the glory of her ancestral tradition of courage and patronage of arts.

In 1542, she was married to Dalpatshah, the eldest son of king Sangramshah of Gond Dynasty. Chandel and Gond dynasties got closer as a consequence of this marriage and that was the reason Keerat Rai got the help of Gonds and his son-in-law Dalpatshah at the time of invasion of Shershah Suri in which Shershah Suri died.

She gave birth to a son in 1545 A.D. who was named Vir Narayan. Dalpatshah died in about 1550 A.D. As Vir Narayan was too young at that time, Durgavati took the reins of the Gond kingdom in her hands. Two ministers Adhar Kayastha and Man Thakur helped the Rani in looking after the administration successfully and effectively. Rani moved her capital to Chauragarh in place of Singaurgarh. It was a fort of strategic importance situated on the Satpura hill range.

After the death of Shershah, Sujat Khan captured the Malwa zone and was succeeded by his son Bajbahadur in 1556 A.D. (Bajbahadur is famous in history for his tumultus love affair with Rani Roopmati). After ascending to the throne, he attacked Rani Durgavati but the attack was repulsed with heavy losses to his army. This defeat effectively silenced Bajbahadur and the victory brought name and fame for Rani Durgavati.

In the year 1562 Akbar vanquished the Malwa ruler Baj Bahadur and annexed the Malwa with Mughul dominion. Consequently, the state boundary of Rani touched the Mughal kingdom.

Rani's contemporary Mughul Subedar was Abdul Mazid Khan, an ambitious man who vanquished Ramchandra, the ruler of Rewa. Prosperity of Rani Durgavati's state lured him and he invaded Rani's state after taking permission from Mughul emperor. This plan of Mughul invasion was the result of expansionism and imperialism of Akbar.

When Rani heard about the attack by Asaf Khan she decide to defend her kingdom with all her might although her minister Adhar pointed out the strength of Mughal forces. Rani maintained that it was better to die respectfully than to live a disgraceful life.

To fight a defensive battle, she went to Narrai situated between a hilly range on one side and two rivers Gaur and Narmada on the other side. It was an unequal battle with trained soldiers and modern weapons in multitude on one side and a few untrained soldiers with old weapons on the other side. Her Fauzdar Arjun Daswas killed in the battle and Rani decided to lead the defence herself. As the enemy entered the valley, soldiers of Rani attacked them. Both sides lost some men but Rani was victorious in this battle. She chased the Mughul army and came out of the valley.

At this stage Rani reviewed her strategy with her counsellors. She wanted to attack the enemy in the night to enfeeble them but her lieutenants did not accept her suggestion. By next morning Asaf khan had summoned big guns. Rani rode on her elephant Sarman and came for the battle. Her son Vir Narayan also took part in this battle. He forced Mughul army to move back three times but at last he got wounded and had to retire to a safe place. In the course of battle Rani also got injured near her ear with an arrow. Another arrow pierced her neck and she lost her consciousness. On regaining consciousness she perceived that defeat was imminent. Her Mahout advised her to leave the battlefield but she refused and took out her dagger and killed herself. Her martyrdom day(24th June 1564) is even today commomorated as "Balidan Diwas".

Rani Durgavati's was a personality with varied facets. She was valiant, beautiful and brave and also a great leader with administrative skills. Her self-respect forced her to fight till death rather than surrender herself to her enemy.

She, like her ancestral dynasty, built so many lakes in her state and did a lot for the welfare of her people. She respected the scholars and extended her patronage to them. She welcomed the Vitthalnath of Vallabh community and took Diksha from him. She was secular and appointed many eminent Muslims on important posts.

The place where she sacrificed herself has always been a source of inspiration for freedom fighters.

In the year 1983, the Government of Madhya Pradesh renamed the University of Jabalpur as Rani Durgavati Vishwavidyalaya in her memory.

Government of India paid its tribute to the valiant Rani by issuing a postal-stamp commemorating her martyrdom, on 24th June 1988.

FIVE

RANI CHENNABHAIRADEVI

BENGALURU: Stories of kings and queens always attract the young and the old alike. Indian history is abundant with interesting tales of brave queens. In India, where women strive to emulate Sita, and are often docile and meekly submit without resisting , there were valiant women taking up arms against enemies and often succeeded in their attempts. One such brave ruler was Rani Chennabhairadevi, the queen of Gerusoppa, who ruled for 54 years — the longest reign by any Indian woman ruler.

Gerusoppa, situated on the banks of the river Sharavathi in Uttara Kannada, was under the control of the Vijayanagara kings. In the decentralised Vijayanagara empire, various regions were ruled by royal families known as Mahamandaleshwaras. By the early 1550s, Chennabhairadevi, who belonged to the Saluva dynasty, became the queen. As per the inscriptions, her kingdom extended from south of Goa to Uttara Kannada, Dakshina Kannada and Malabar. This region is known not only for harbours like Bhatkala, Honnavar, Mirjan, Ankola and Baindur but also for pepper.

Honnavar and Bhatkala served as internal and international, flourishing trading centres. Arabian horses and weapons were imported from the West. Pepper, betel nut and nutmeg were exported to European and Arab countries. Chennabhairadevi found herself at confrontation with the neighbouring rival kingdoms as well as the Portuguese. The attempts of the Keladi kings and Bilgi chieftains to pull the queen down proved futile.

The queen had to resist the Portuguese who tried to grab the ports and take over the trade. She was at war with the Portuguese in 1559 and again in

1570. She crushed the Portuguese army with her intelligent battle strategy. One of the Portuguese chronicles states that during the war of 1570, the Portuguese attacked Honnavar and burnt it to the ground. After the decline of Vijayanagar, Chennabhairadevi dealt with the Portuguese diplomatically, who nicknamed her 'Raina de Pimenta' — the Pepper Queen.

SIX

RANI AVANTIBAI

Not much is known about Rani Avantibai who is, today, honoured as a warrior queen and an important, inspirational figure in the history of the Indian freedom struggle – notably, the 1857 War of Independence. Very little has been written about her. Steadfast in her loyalty to her people and throne, Rani Avantibai is an icon of rebellion, sacrifice and martyrdom in a long, brutal history of fighting colonial rule. This is her story.

Early Life

Avantibai was born on 16 August 1831 into a zamindar family. She is known to have been extremely independent and well trained in her childhood years. She was not only skilled in military strategy and state affairs but was also fully capable of archery, horse-riding and wielding a sword.

Her political and combat education made her a good candidate for a ruler. With word spreading about her skills and charismatic personality across the Narmada Valley, she was accepted as a suitable bride for the king's son. At a young age (c.1849) she was married to Vikramaditya Lodhi of Ramgarh (which presently lies in Madhya Pradesh).

Given how accomplished and well-suited she was for taking over the throne, it is no surprise that when her husband became too ill to continue ruling, she was the one who took over in his stead. Although her kingdom flourished under her rule, the British did not approve of her sitting on her husband's throne.

Court of Wards

After the king fell ill, the British refused to accept Avantibai's sons (Aman Singh and Sher Singh) as legitimate heirs to the throne, given that they were minors. Seeing as, in their eyes, there was no heir to the Ramgarh throne, it allowed them to install their own administration to replace the Lodhi rule.

Image Source: InUth

This was due to a fairly ambiguous annexation policy (the Doctrine of Lapse, commonly associated with Lord Dalhousie) that was applied by the British East India Company before 1858. It allowed the Company to install administration in any princely state if the ruler was incompetent or died without a male heir – taking away Indian rulers' rights to appoint successors.

On 13 September 1851, Ramgargh was declared the Court of Wards with a British-approved administrator – Sheikh Mohammad – installed in place. This decision did not sit well with Rani Avantibai. Deeply insulted by this act of the British East India Company, she bided her time until she could retaliate.

After the king's death in 1857, she found the perfect opportunity to respond to the foreign insult. She had the administrator thrown out of the kingdom and declared war upon British rule.

The 1857 Rebellion

By May 1857, news about the incidents in Meerut and Delhi had spread across the subcontinent. For months, people in villages had been preparing for a rebellion after the news of rifles using cow and pig fat began to make rounds. Rani Avantibai, too, decided to send her own message.

Carrying handwritten notes and a set of bangles, emissaries were sent to neighbouring kingdoms to gain support in the war against the British. The message – if they had any semblance of loyalty or honour towards their country, they would pick up arms and fight – or they could sit at home and wear those bangles.

Also Read: Rani Abbakka Chowta: The Queen Who Made Portuguese Colonisers Miserable | #IndianWomenInHistory

After an incident where the British caught a whiff of rebellion and executed King Shankar Shah, the entire region was incensed and ready to fight back. Rani Avantibai's own people relied on her to become the leader of the rebellion. Her influence had multiple central provinces joining her armed fight. She raised an army of 4000 people, leading them to the war.

The statue of Rani Avantibai at Dongagarh, Chhattisgarh. Image Source: Wikimedia Commons

Rani Avantibai in battle

Rani Avantibai led her troops to a village named Kheri, near Mandla. While the British expected an easy victory, they were shocked to be defeated by her army. They had no choice but to back down while she controlled Mandla from December 1857 to February 1858.

The British did not take this slight with grace. Determined to wipe out her rule, they retaliated with brutal force and attacked Ramgarh – and no amount of passionate patriotism and love for her people could stop them from crushing her army with military strength. They set the region on fire and Rani Avantibai had no choice but to seek safety in the hilly forests of Devharigarh.

Still, the queen did not give up. Utilising guerrilla warfare techniques, she infiltrated General Waddington's camp and disbanded his forces. Unfortunately, a fighting spirit was not enough against sheer battle power. Eventually, she found herself trapped by British forces, who had surrounded Ramgarh. Knowing that her defeat was imminent, she found it better to sacrifice her life than to be taken at the hands of the enemy.

On 20th March 1858, she fell upon her own sword and became a martyr. Her last words are said to have been: "हमारी दुरूगावती ने जीते जी वैरी के हाथ से अंग न छुए जाने का प्रण लिया था. इसे न भूलना बडो" (Our Durgavati vowed to never let the enemy get their hands on her while she lived. Don't forget this).

Legacy

While Rani Avantibai's story did not necessarily make it to mainstream narratives, it continued to live through local folklore, theatre performances and written across the official documents and writings that recorded the events of that time.

SEVEN
VELU NACHIYAR

A warrior queen, a gallant female military commander and an army of 5000 - together they gave the British a tough time! This was a historic event that gave India not only its first female warrior but also involved what is said to be the first-ever instance of suicide bombing in India.

During the 18th century, in the Sivagangai estate in present-day Tamil Nadu, there lived a Queen named Velu Nachiyar. Velu was the only daughter of the Royal couple of the Sethupathi Dynasty and was raised as the Royal heir. Trained in martial arts, horse riding and archery, she could also speak several languages including French, Urdu, and English.

The turning point in Velu's life was when the British - led by the son of the Nawab of Arcot - killed her husband Muthu Vaduganatha Thevar in the Kalaiyar Koil War. Velu and her daughter, Vellachi, were then forced to flee from Sivagangai.

Velu reached Dindigul, a distant land from Sivagangai where she spent eight years under the sanctuary of the then ruler of Dindigul - Gopal Naicker.

It was at Dindigul that she also met Haider Ali, the Sultan of Mysore, in whose eyes she found favour as she had impressed him with her fluent Urdu and intellect.

In 1780, with the unwavering support of Gopal Naicker and allied forces of Haider Ali, Velu Nachiyar set out to avenge her beloved's death and regain control over her kingdom.

While the British had taken complete control over the Sivaganga Fort, in Dindigul, Velu along with her military commander, Kuyuili, devised a suicide plan. For the plan to be successful, it was important to know where the British had stored their arms and ammunition. With Velu's excellent sources of intelligence, she gathered agents who helped her find the armoury chambers in the fort and soon, the plan was set to action.

Velu Nachiyar on a 2008 commemorative postal stamp of India.

On the day of Vijayadashami, Kuyuili and a few other women set out to the Fort. On Kuyuili's command, the women poured ghee on her and drenched in it, Kuyuili fearlessly walked into the armoury chamber and set herself on fire, destroying each weapon that was stored there.

Following Kuyuili's sacrifice, Velu launched an attack on the Fort with the aim of taking over her Kingdom. Velu not only fought the British but also the Nawab of Arcot, fearlessly and full of valour and this earned her the title, 'Veeramangai' - the brave one.

www.ingramcontent.com/pod-product-compliance
Lightning Source LLC
Chambersburg PA
CBHW072146150726
48002CB00004B/1655